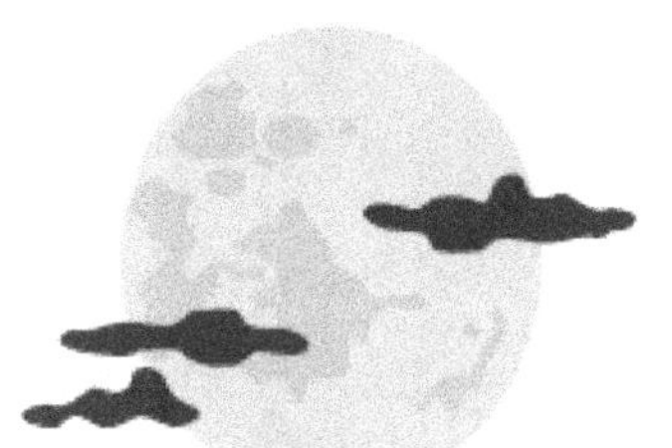

THIS BOOK BELONGS TO:

WOULD YOU RATHER
go to a really great
Halloween party where
you did not know
anyone
OR
WOULD YOU RATHER
go to a kind of lame
Halloween party
where you knew
almost everyone
there

WOULD YOU RATHER

win a contest for
having the best
costume

WOULD YOU RATHER

win a contest for
making the best
jack-o-lantern

WOULD YOU RATHER

have to sleep in
a coffin

OR

WOULD YOU RATHER

have to live in
a giant pumpkin

WOULD YOU RATHER

have to eat 6 fish eyeballs

WOULD YOU RATHER

have to eat a small frog

WOULD YOU RATHER
have to wear your
Halloween costume to
school every day until
thanksgiving
OR
WOULD YOU RATHER
have to wear a
jack-o-lantern over
your head to school
for the first three
days of November

WOULD YOU RATHER

help to design and make a
haunted
house

 **OR**

WOULD YOU RATHER

go to a haunted house
that someone
else has created

WOULD YOU RATHER

be chased by
five zombies

OR

WOULD YOU RATHER

be chased by
one werewolf

WOULD YOU RATHER

trick-or-treat in a
neighborhood

WOULD YOU RATHER

trick-or-treat
at a mall

WOULD YOU RATHER

eat all of your
Halloween candy

OR

WOULD YOU RATHER

trade your Halloween
candy for $10

WOULD YOU RATHER

dress up as a devil

WOULD YOU RATHER

dress up as an angel

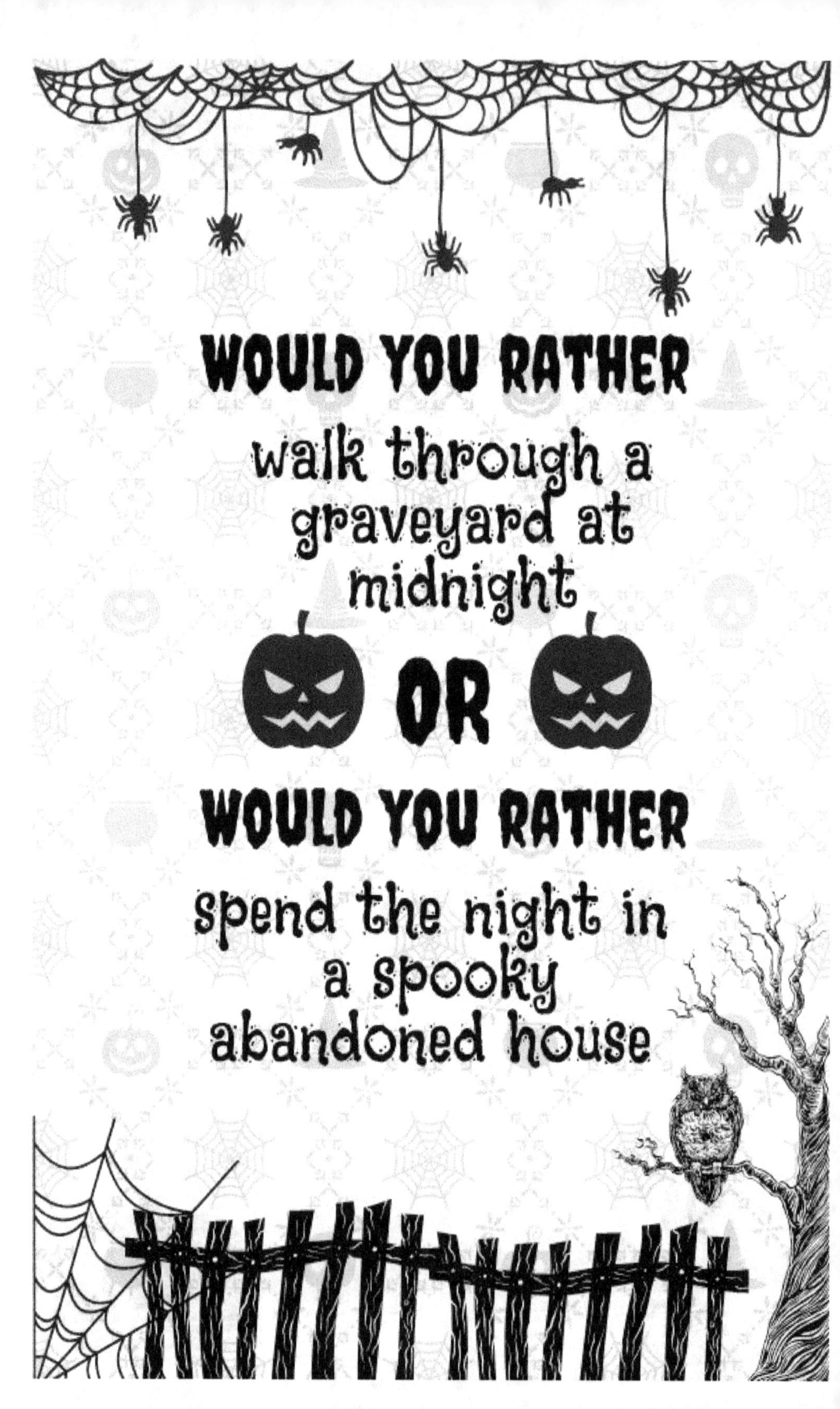

WOULD YOU RATHER
walk through a graveyard at midnight
OR
WOULD YOU RATHER
spend the night in a spooky abandoned house

WOULD YOU RATHER

Be locked in a
room full
of snakes

WOULD YOU RATHER

Be locked in a room
full of rats

WOULD YOU RATHER

Face a Zombie
Apocalypse

OR

WOULD YOU RATHER

an Invasion of
10-ft spiders

WOULD YOU RATHER

Take an evening
swim at Amity Cove

 **OR**

WOULD YOU RATHER

a midnight stroll
in a cemetery

WOULD YOU RATHER

Dress up as a
character from
Harry Potter

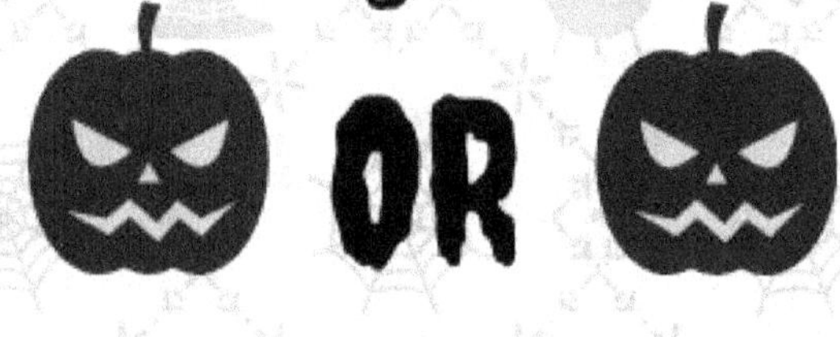

OR

WOULD YOU RATHER

Dress up as a
character from
Star wars

WOULD YOU RATHER
Wait for the Great Pumpkin with Linus

WOULD YOU RATHER

celebrate Christmas with Jack Skellington

WOULD YOU RATHER

Live a world where
King Kong

WOULD YOU RATHER

Live a world where
Megalodon are real

WOULD YOU RATHER

Have a nightmare featuring the clown Pennywise

OR

WOULD YOU RATHER

the Headless Horseman

WOULD YOU RATHER

walk through a
graveyard at
midnight

OR

WOULD YOU RATHER

spend the night in
a spooky
abandoned house

WOULD YOU RATHER

Have vampire teeth

WOULD YOU RATHER

a witch's mole
on your nose

WOULD YOU RATHER

Be a member of
the Brady Bunch

OR

WOULD YOU RATHER

the Addams' Family

WOULD YOU RATHER

dunk for apples

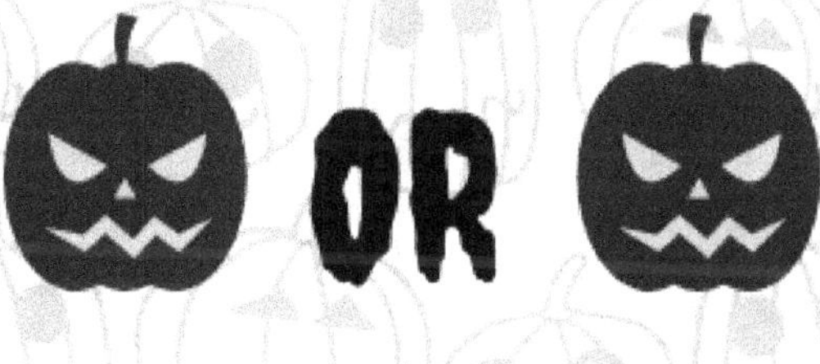 OR

WOULD YOU RATHER

carve a jack-lantern

WOULD YOU RATHER

eat a caramel apple

 **OR**

WOULD YOU RATHER

a caramel popcorn ball

WOULD YOU RATHER
Light a bonfire

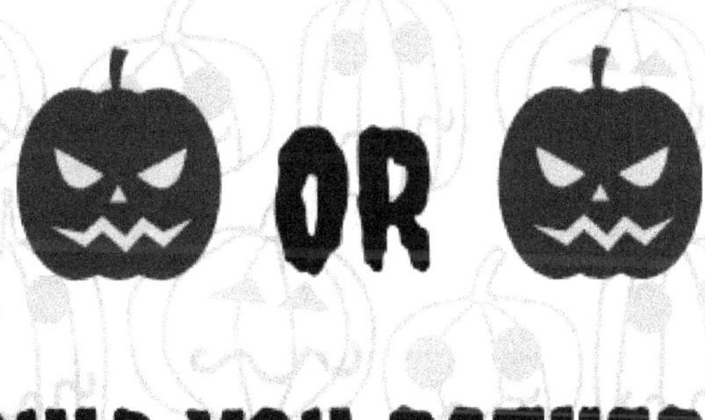 **OR**

WOULD YOU RATHER

a candle at the graves of the dead

WOULD YOU RATHER
Eat pumpkin
pie

WOULD YOU RATHER

apple cider
donuts

WOULD YOU RATHER
Stay at the Hotel Transylvania

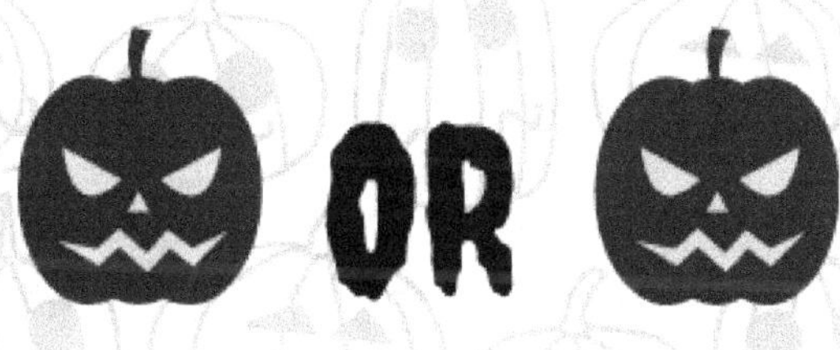

WOULD YOU RATHER

the Monster House

WOULD YOU RATHER

Ride the Tower of Terror

WOULD YOU RATHER

the Haunted Mansion

WOULD YOU RATHER

Live in the world
of A Quiet Place

WOULD YOU RATHER

Hocus Pocus

WOULD YOU RATHER

Create a monster like
Frankenstein

WOULD YOU RATHER

become one like
Dr Jekyll

WOULD YOU RATHER

Fall into a pool of blood

WOULD YOU RATHER

walk through a graveyard at midnight

WOULD YOU RATHER

Stay home to
give out candy

OR

WOULD YOU RATHER

go
trick-or-treating

WOULD YOU RATHER
Attend a sexy Halloween party

WOULD YOU RATHER

visit New England for the Autumn leaves

WOULD YOU RATHER

meet a vampire

WOULD YOU RATHER

meet a werewolf

WOULD YOU RATHER

Ride the Tower of Terror

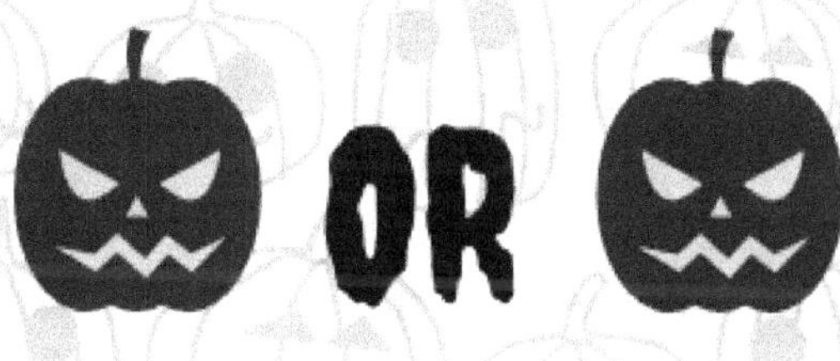

OR

WOULD YOU RATHER

the Haunted Mansion

WOULD YOU RATHER

eat a live
cockroach

OR

WOULD YOU RATHER

play a game
of Ouija

WOULD YOU RATHER

read a spooky story

WOULD YOU RATHER

see a spooky movie

WOULD YOU RATHER

have a homemade
costume

WOULD YOU RATHER

have a store-bought
costume

WOULD YOU RATHER

get 20 of your favorite treats on Halloween

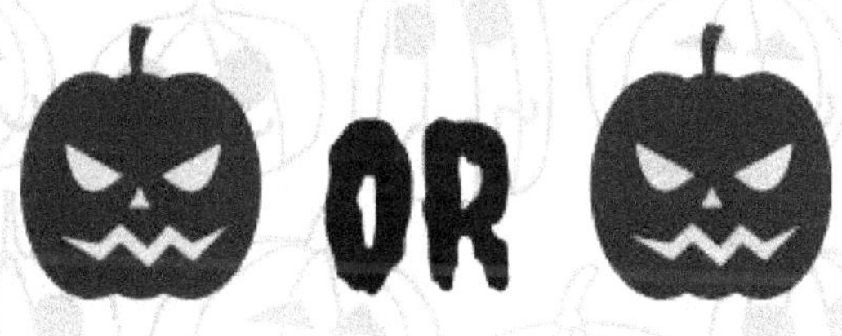

WOULD YOU RATHER

get 50 treats that are not your favorites on Halloween

WOULD YOU RATHER

be a vampire

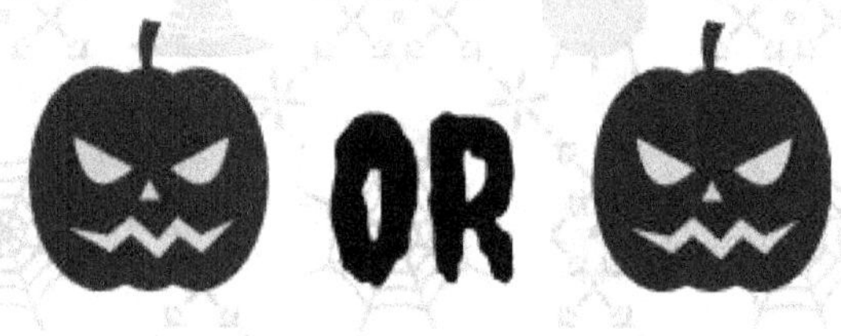 **OR**

WOULD YOU RATHER

be a werewolf

WOULD YOU RATHER

go trick-or-treating
with a group of
friends

OR

WOULD YOU RATHER

get paid $20 to take
a little kid
trickor-treating

WOULD YOU RATHER

WOULD YOU RATHER

WOULD YOU RATHER

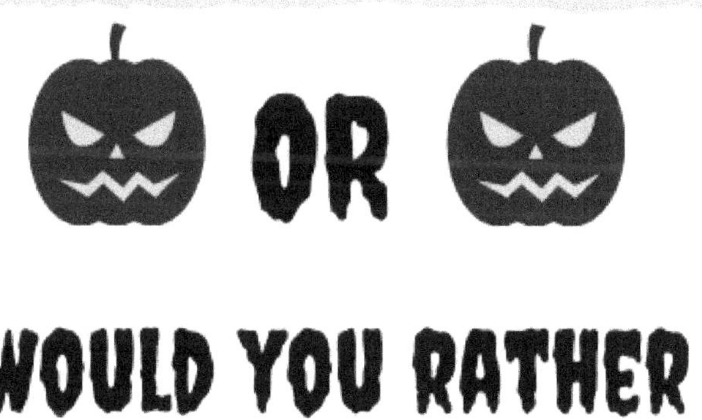

OR

WOULD YOU RATHER

WOULD YOU RATHER

____

____

WOULD YOU RATHER

____

____

WOULD YOU RATHER

WOULD YOU RATHER

WOULD YOU RATHER

OR

WOULD YOU RATHER

WOULD YOU RATHER

WOULD YOU RATHER

WOULD YOU RATHER

WOULD YOU RATHER

WOULD YOU RATHER

WOULD YOU RATHER

WOULD YOU RATHER

 **OR** 

WOULD YOU RATHER

WOULD YOU RATHER

OR

WOULD YOU RATHER